HOW TO

MANAGE YOUR

NARCISSISTIC

BOSS

Effectively Manage Narcissists At Work, Deal With Difficult Personalities, Overcome Your Narcissistic Employers And Achieve Success In The Workplace

PAUL J. EDWARDS

TABLE OF CONTENTS

Paul J. Edwards

THIS PAGE IS INTENTIONALLY
LEFT BLANK

INTRODUCTION

I welcome you all to a transformative journey of **how to manage your narcissistic boss.** The rate at which narcissistic bosses can create a hostile work environment that impedes personal development, teamwork, and overall performance in today's fast-paced and competitive professional setting is quite destructive and this can be extremely alarming.

This book is your definitive guide to conquering workplace narcissism, overcoming your narcissistic boss and taking charge of your destiny with confidence and empowerment. In this book you will gain access to priceless knowledge about comprehending, recognizing, and successfully dealing with narcissistic bosses in the workplace. We will also together, go deeply into the psychology of narcissism to assist you in differentiating between constructive confidence and damaging egocentrism. But that's not all.

As we continue on this journey you'll also find a potent selection of tactics and tried-and-true methods to speak assertively, set clear limits, the art of conflict resolution and adeptly handling difficult colleagues, as well as practical self-preservation techniques to help you protect yourself from emotional manipulation.

We will also be studying some real-life case studies of both triumphs and challenges that emanates from narcissistic bosses and workplace narcissism and it would offer you a relatable context to internalize and apply the strategies discussed.

I assure you that by the time you reach the final pages of this transformative book, you will have gained a profound understanding of managing narcissistic bosses at work as well as dealing with workplace narcissism, and you will be adequately-prepared to thrive in all manners of challenging workplace scenario.

Are you ready to become the master of your workplace life and professional destiny? Let's take it HEAD ON.

UNDERSTANDING NARCISSISM

Welcome to the very beginning of this journey, in this chapter we will be discussing the term narcissism in order for us to be able to differentiate between it and constructive confidence.

(NPD) Narcissistic Personality Disorder

This is a mental health condition that is characterized by lack of empathy, superiority-complex, manipulative motives, a huge sense of grandiosity, and a constant and strong desire for the spotlight and praise.

A narcissist is someone who has a strong desire to be always be the center of attention and attraction, to be seen always as the best by others, always praised for their accomplishments and unable to make mistakes. A narcissistic boss would always blame you for his misdeeds and mistakes, take credit for your works and achievements, take advantage of you if given the opportunity and would always want you to believe that they are special, the best and that they deserve all the credits.

Narcissism can manifest on a spectrum, ranging from mild traits to a full-blown personality disorder. I will implore you to note that having some narcissistic tendencies doesn't necessarily make someone a narcissist. As humans we all possess varying degrees of self-centeredness and some other narcissistic traits, and the only time it begins to get problematic is when we begin to allow these traits whether knowingly or not dominate our behavior and impair our relationships.

Narcissistic tendencies in persons most times start from childhood. A narcissistic personality most likely grew up in an environment where they felt neglected, unimportant, or lacked genuine emotional support and then they begin to develop a coping mechanism that revolves around self-centeredness to protect themselves from further emotional harm. So whenever we are dealing with a narcissist it is very important that we do so empathically and with adequate understanding of their situation because as said earlier it is as much as a mental disorder.

But then despite the situation that brought about the traits in these individuals, working with narcissists especially when that person's your boss can be very exhausting

A narcissistic boss might necessitate excessive and unnecessary praises, manipulative and purposely ignoring you and your work achievements. He/she will most likely want things at your own expense and would go for it without batting an eyelid.

People with narcissistic tendencies can find it very hard to have real and caring relationships. Taking your narcissistic boss for an example; the relationship between you and he/she would always be that of a wicked boss and a hating employee. Now imagine if this was also the kind of relationship that exists amongst all employees and their bosses, the world would definitely be a disaster.

Narcissist finds it difficult to get meaningful relationships with people because the traits inherent in them makes them to focus too much on themselves and don't understand how others feel. It's like they're looking in a mirror that only shows their reflection and not the people around them.

Narcissism, beyond the way it is portrayed by the public, is more of an intricate tapestry of human complexity, woven with both light and darkness. To truly grasp its essence, we must venture beyond the surface and unlock the hidden chambers that few have glimpsed.

The journey has begun, and as you have taken this first step, you won't be able to resist the magnetic pull of this captivating exploration. Fasten your seat-belt as we delve into the intrinsic layers self-discovery and understanding that will forever reshape your perceptions and understanding of narcissism and you would also get equipped with the easy ways to dealing with your narcissistic boss in the workplace

SIGNS YOUR BOSS IS A NARCISSIST

In this chapter we will be focusing on understanding the signs to watch out for to know if our boss is a narcissist is and how we can recognize it.

It is important to note that it is just very normal to come across bosses and employers with selfish motives, self-confidence and esteem and toxic personalities, so how do you recognize when you are dealing with a narcissistic boss and differentiate them from these set of persons. Let's check these out.

- Sense of self or self-centeredness: narcissistic bosses often talk and think about themselves most of if not all of the time. They are always conscious of their appearances, wealth, accomplishments, gifts, skills, talents and others that deem fit. They will never hesitate to tell anyone and everyone about these not caring about your disposition. They do these expecting you to give them attention always.

- Inflated sense of importance: as said earlier, narcissistic bosses will tell you all the good things about themselves but most times their comments and tales are not necessarily true and are most times inflated and exaggerated.
- Success fantasies: most narcissistic bosses always tend to always

fantasize success, power and wealth, and because of these fantasies they begin to believe they deserve the very best of everything.

- Sense of entitlement: narcissists always think that they are meant to be favored above others. They believe that others are existing primarily to serve and meet their needs and they don't care about the wants, desires and feelings the others. They believe that they should be offered special favor by others and that they should satisfy and fulfill their requests without questioning them. When the victim of a narcissist does not give the narcissist these treatments, the narcissist tends to become impatient, angry and defensive and may resort to giving the other the silent treatment.

- Manipulative tendencies: narcissists are the kind of persons who easily draw people towards themselves though hard to maintain such persons but they tend to attract people due to the way they present themselves as confident, unyielding and charismatic. Narcissistic bosses tend to be manipulative and as such they can go at any length to make those under them to do their bidding even if it is to the extent of burnout and work stress.

They may appear subtle at the approach but after successfully influencing their victims they begin to control them without their victims recognizing it.

- Requires constant praises: narcissists are people who always feel fear, insecure and vulnerable and they have a very fragile self-esteem and this is the main factor that builds the NPD traits in them. Narcissistic bosses might require constant praises and eulogies due to their fragile self-esteem as they need the praises to prop themselves up.
- Envy: a narcissistic boss who have employees or subordinates that own things or possess qualities they don't

will always be envious of such person due to their sense of low self-esteem. They may even begin to see these persons as threats and will always work to get those things and won't bother to bring down whoever seems to be in their way.

- They lack empathy: narcissistic bosses are never empathetic and always have struggles in empathizing with others.
- They are incredibly charming: as said earlier people are drawn towards narcissists as they present themselves in a very charming way due to their feeling of superiority and self-importance. People get attracted to them and are perceived as incredible at the first impression but as they progress

in the relationship they are no longer perceived as such as their narcissistic traits begins to manifest visibly and they become maligning and sometimes aggressive towards others.

- Extremely competitive
- Hold grudges
- Hates being criticized
- Extremely ambitious

These are quite the main key pointers you are working with a narcissistic boss or employer and note that the process of identifying these traits requires a requisite deal of patience to avoid a faulty and wrong conclusion on your boss's personality.

Paul J. Edwards

THE IMPACT OF A NARCISSISTIC BOSS ON WORKPLACE DYNAMICS

In the bustling world of work today, the presence of narcissism can create a web of complexities, influencing both individuals and the overall team dynamics. Narcissism at work can really be a thorn in the flesh, especially when the narcissist is your boss. In this chapter we will be delving into the hidden effects of a narcissistic boss in the dynamics of the workplace.

The most prominent impact of a narcissistic boss in the workplace is toxic atmosphere and difficult environment. Narcissistic behavior can cast a shadow over the workplace, creating a toxic atmosphere that stifles productivity. The constant need for attention and validation from narcissistic boss can dampens morale and lead to power struggles, making the workplace feel like a battleground where the fittest and most powerful survives. The presence of a narcissistic boss can eliminate the unique quality of the workplace as a harmonious environment.

Team Division also is very inherent with the presence of a narcissistic boss. Narcissistic personalities tends to prioritize their own needs and achievements and this can drive a wedge between team members, narcissistic bosses may exploit or undermine their subordinates or employees to elevate themselves thereby creating hatred and animosity within the team.

Narcissists are naturally self-centered and as such they can hinder collaboration and open communication. Workers or subordinates of a narcissistic boss may hesitate to share ideas or concerns, fearing potential backlash from the narcissistic boss and this can stifle creativity and innovation.

The constant need for attention and admiration may distract narcissists from their actual work responsibilities and this can lead to low productivity in the workplace.

Moreover, working with a narcissistic boss can be emotionally draining for staffs. The manipulation and lack of empathy from the narcissistic boss can lead to feelings of frustration, stress, and even burnout among workers.

The toxic atmosphere created by a narcissistic boss may lead to a high employee turnover rate or brain drain. Talented staffs may be forced to seek opportunities elsewhere to escape the negative environment and these results to a loss of valuable expertise and skills for the organization.

A narcissistic in leadership positions may prioritize their own interests over the organization's goals, leading to poor decision-making and a lack of focus on the team's well-being and organizational visions.

The manipulative behavior of narcissistic bosses can erode trust within the

[24]

team. Workers of a narcissistic boss may become skeptical of the boss's intentions and question their motives, making it challenging to build strong working relationships between the staffs and the boss.

A narcissistic boss will continually refuse feedbacks or criticism from his staffs or competitors as he will see it as a form of attack on his fragile self-esteem. This resistance can hinder personal and professional growth and prevent them from learning and improving and thus affecting the productivity rate of the organization.

Understanding the impact of narcissism on workplace dynamics and the way having a narcissistic leader can affect the workplace allows us as individuals and organizations to take proactive steps to address and mitigate

its effects and create a thriving workplace

where everyone can reach their full potential.

THE IMPACT OF A NARCISSISTIC BOSS ON YOUR MENTAL HEALTH

Apart from the fact that narcissistic leaders have a great deal of impact on the dynamics of the workplace, they can also affect the mental health and well-being of their staffs.

Narcissistic bosses believes that they deserve all of the best and that they are always right in whatever they do and if you as a subordinate staff or any other person challenge or corrects them or does not meet their expectation, they begin to see such individual as a threat and the victim would begin to notice foul moods, agitations and irritations. The narcissistic boss could even start to create walls of threats, bully and isolation around such person.

To show their superiority, they may even increase the workload of this person, creating burnout and stress for the person and even when the person manages to completes the work, the narcissistic boss might decide to just ignore or condemn the person's work and might even compare the person's work to that of a younger staff just to belittle and make the fellow feel worthless, forcing the fellow to either wallow in such feeling or quit the job.

Victims of such might then begin to doubt their essence in the organization, their professional prowess, works, achievements and their ability to even move up or maintain their current position.

These set of persons could then begin to think on and wallow in these doubts and the level of uncertainties begins to escalate and they begin to undermine their productivity and self-esteem.

The truth of the whole matter is that having a narcissistic boss is not always a good thing due to the negative, psychological and emotional warfare they use to ensure they get admiration, respect and their position at work.

The entire organization suffers when there is a narcissistic leader both professionally and psychological therefore making it important for you to always check yourself in order to maintain your emotional and mental well-being all of which will be opened to you as you continue with this book.

Paul J. Edwards

DEALING

WITH A

NARCISSISTIC

BOSS

KNOW YOUR VALUE

The first thing to note after understanding and recognizing narcissism and the impacts a narcissistic boss can have on both your mental health and workplace dynamics is to recognize your worth.

In recognizing your value, you can first of all think about the reason you were employed in the first place. This is not always easy but with certain set of people around you it would be made much easier.

Reflect on your qualifications, skills, previous achievements, references and other things that got you landed in that prized position. Remember that the value you give yourself is all up to you and not in anyone's hands but you so the worth you deem fit for yourself is your actual worth.

COMPLEMENT THEM

You practically can't continue to work with a narcissistic boss without this. Narcissists require constant praise and attention.

Once you give yourself to complementing your boss frequently you will be in their good books and would barely be a victim of their bad sides.

They would practically begin to come to you for these accolades whenever they feel down and you will probably even get elevated by this boss in your place of work.

DOCUMENT EVERYTHING

I t is also very important to keep a paper or digital trail of important conversations and interactions with the narcissistic boss. This documentation can serve as evidence if issues escalate, they would help in protecting your interests and providing clarity in challenging situations.

Keeping documented records of your respectful responds to any criticism on any of your works or accomplishments will also help you in retaining your self-esteem and feeling of empowerment and these would help you from being held back from pursuing future goals.

Times could come when situations tend to escalate and would have to be settled by maybe the HR of your organization and in such situations, having documented evidences could always give you a stronger edge over others.

Taking a voiced or video recording of the conversation is not advised as it most likely would be without your boss's knowledge and this action can be illegal in certain territories so a detailed record of dates and details can be just enough.

It could also get to a point in which you will need to take drastic legal actions against the

narcissistic boss or the organization and
having these records will be able to stand as
evidences to support your claims.

NETWORK FOR YOURSELF

When we talk about networking in this context, it simply means creating and keeping contacts with top officials, senior staffs or other leaders within the particular organization.

Networking as explained here is a very easy but delicate step to take as you must ensure that the narcissistic boss you are dealing with is not aware of this step.

You might begin to wonder why it is very important that the narcissistic boss is kept in the dark of this and I will be giving you some reasons why it must be as such.

Narcissists have very fragile self-esteem and they tend to always feel insecure and afraid and that is why they developed narcissistic traits though sometimes unaware of the negative effects it could have on them. Now when your narcissistic boss gets wind that you have actually taken this kind of step he begins to feel insecure around you and views you as a threat.

Taking this step is very delicate but also very essential for your own rising and fulfilling of your professional aspirations.

TAKE NOTE OF WHOM YOU ARE DEALING WITH

Taking note of the personality you are dealing with will help you a great deal in dealing with your narcissistic boss.

Narcissists are individuals who always feel vulnerable, afraid and they also lack self-esteem. When you begin to take into cognizance that you are actually dealing with a fearful, vulnerable and easily wounded lion who is actually carrying within himself a huge load of inferiority which he is ever fighting and trying to conceal then you will actually easily triumph over them.

Regularly remind yourself that your boss is actually very vulnerable than you are and is only trying to conceal it by being manipulative and controlling.

In fact, when you begin to look at things from this factual point of view you will begin to treat them with empathy as you might literally begin to feel pity for them.

DEVELOPING ALLIANCE STRATEGY

Narcissistic bosses have those who are suppliers and those who are injurers. Whenever a narcissistic boss has a narcissistic injury they always look for people to praise and complement them, so it is also important that you position yourself as an ally when working with a narcissistic boss.

SETTING BOUNDARIES

Boundaries can stand as invisible fences that protect your emotional, mental psychological and physical space. The process of setting boundaries while dealing with a narcissistic boss involves the clear communication of your values, needs, limits, norms and ethics to them. By doing this, you establish guidelines for how you wish to be treated and what you will be able to tolerate while working with them and in different situations.

In communicating your boundaries to your boss the first thing you need is to be aware of the things you can accept from them. You should first reflect on your emotions and what makes you feel uncomfortable or stressed and this in turn will help you recognize situations where boundaries are necessary

Secondly you need to know that you are actually dealing with your boss and it requires that you express your boundaries calmly and assertively. Always use "I" statements to communicate your needs as well as those boundaries and ensure you don't blame them while doing so.

Also, ensure to stay firm in maintaining your boundaries as consistency is the key that reinforces your self-respect and lets your narcissistic boss and others know you are serious about those boundaries

In order to make your boss and others respect your space, you must encourage mutual respect by respecting their boundaries as well

Furthermore, you need to learn how to say "No": Saying "no" when necessary is not selfish but it is actually a way to protect your well-being and privacy. Prioritize your needs when dealing with a narcissistic boss and don't feel guilty about putting yourself first because it is a need.

MAINTAINING YOUR WELL-BEING WHILE DEALING WITH A NARCISSISTIC BOSS

M anaging narcissistic bosses can be emotionally and psychologically challenging especially in a workplace setting when you have no say in your boss's life and character, but you can safeguard your well-being by adopting strategies that promote resilience and self-care.

In maintaining your well-being you need to create time for self-care activities that rejuvenate your mind and body. You can engage in hobbies, exercise, or meditation can help in boosting your emotional resilience.

You can also reach out to trusted friends, family, or support groups to share your experiences and seek comfort. Having a strong emotional support system can help you cope with this challenging situation.

Moreover, know that it's okay to feel overwhelmed, and you are not responsible for your boss's behaviors therefore be kind to yourself and practice self-compassion.

Also learn to adjust your expectations and goals when dealing with a narcissistic boss. You should also realize that their behavior may not change, and your focus should be on self-preservation.

Furthermore, whenever it is possible, try as much as possible to minimize contact with toxic and negative persons. Surround yourself with positive influences (persons and things, visible and invisible) that will uplift and support you.

Also, accept that you cannot change the narcissist's behavior. Instead, focus on how you respond and how you protect your well-being.

You should also try to always acknowledge and celebrate your resilience in managing challenging situations. Recognize and celebrate your strengths and achievements.

In addition, writing can be therapeutic and help you gain clarity on certain things so you can just keep and write in a journal where process your emotions and reflect on your experiences

Practice mindfulness to stay present and focused on the present moment and it would help reduce stress and promote your emotional well-being.

Lastly, seek professional guidance and help if the emotional toll becomes overwhelming as professional guidance can provide valuable coping strategies.

Remember, you have the power to safeguard your emotional health and lead a more fulfilling life, even in the presence of challenging individuals like a narcissistic boss.

Nurture your inner strength and prioritize self-care and it will enable you to navigate difficult situations with grace and resilience. By embracing these strategies, you can protect your well-being while managing your narcissistic boss.

SEEK SUPPORT AND HELP

Working with a narcissistic boss can take a huge toll on your mental and emotional health and these then makes it of utmost importance to seek help from outside whenever it is needed.

You might begin to feel symptoms of anxiety and depression as you might find that you always take home streams of manipulations of your boss's voice and other actions taken by your narcissistic boss echoing in your head and replaying in your mind. Whenever this happens ensure you visit a professional counselor, doctor or therapist for check-up and help.

It might be challenging to sort through complex emotions on your own. But you can handle these feelings with help and without being judged if you seek support from friends, co-workers and professionals who can offer specialized support and therapy approaches if you encounter ongoing emotional challenges or mental and psychological health issues.

Furthermore, ensure to self-awareness and self-observation. Share whatever you are passing through with friends and families and they would help you walk through it triumphantly through giving you valid points of their own view of your work, relationship with your boss as well as your own character.

Moreover, when you work with a therapist or counselor, you can develop emotionally and have a better knowledge of the kind of personality you carry. This has a favorable effect on your work relationships and wellbeing.

Lastly, seeking help and asking for assistance is not a sign of weakness but actually a show of strength. Therefore practice self-care, self-help and seek outside help. Whether it is from a friend, a counselor, therapist or a support group and watch yourself acquire the strength and compassion you need to deal with the difficulties of working with a narcissistic boss as well as triumphing in the workplace.

WALKING AWAY AND DIVERSIFICATION

Lastly, another thing a person facing a narcissistic boss challenge at work is to walk away.

You can try to diversify your work experience while working you're your narcissistic boss by working with other departments heads and other leaders at your workplace but these kind of opportunities to diversify are not always open to everyone as not all workplace has diverse units

Diversification of work role and experience is also a very useful and tactical way of managing a narcissistic boss as these other leaders and senior staffs you have

[54]

worked with could always stand as your references whenever you want to get another job.

You could also decide to consult a labor law expert as you have the right to a confortable work environment as an employee and when these rights are getting violated you can take legal actions or speak to a labor law expert to get the requisite leverage to move forward.

CONCLUSION

In the pages of "How to Manage Your Narcissistic Boss," we've explored the intricate world of workplace dynamics and provided valuable insights on navigating the challenging terrain of dealing with a narcissistic superior. Throughout this journey, we've learned that understanding, empathy, and strategic communication are powerful tools in our arsenal.

As you close the book, remember that managing a narcissistic boss is not an insurmountable task; it's a skill that can be mastered. By setting boundaries, cultivating self-confidence, and employing the techniques discussed here, you can transform a difficult situation into an opportunity for personal growth and professional success.

So, as you face your narcissistic boss and the challenges they bring, stand tall, equipped with the knowledge and strategies you've acquired. Embrace the power of resilience, adaptability, and self-awareness. Ultimately, the key to success lies in your ability to manage not only your boss but also your own responses to the situation. Your journey to a harmonious and productive workplace begins now, and with determination and a compassionate heart, you can thrive in any professional environment.

NOTES

_____

_____

_____

_____

_____

_____

_____

_____

_____

_____

_____

_____

_____

_____

_____

_____

_____

_____

_____

_____

_____

_____

_____